Wanderi:
A Cultur

Jordan Breed

Copyright © 2024 Jordan Breed
All rights reserved.
Rise2Write Publishing LLC
www.rise2write.com[1]

For information about custom editions, special sales, premium and bulk purchases, please contact:

authorjordanbreed@gmail.com

All rights reserved. No part of this publication may be reproduced, stored in a retrieval system, or transmitted in any form or by any means-for example, electronic, photocopy, recording-without the prior written permission. The only exceptions are brief quotations in printed reviews.

---

1. http://www.rise2write.com

DEDICATION

I dedicate the pocket guidebook to the explorers and the curious minds at heart.

May this guide be your compass as you discover Seattle's vibrant streets, hidden corners, and cultural gems. And to those who find solitude in the journey as much as the destination, this is for you.

Table of Contents

1. Ballard pg. 4-6
2. Beacon Hill pg. 6-8
3. Belltown pg. 8-10
4. Broadview /Bitterlake pg. 11-13
5. Capitol Hill pg. 14-16
6. Central Area pg. 16-19
7. CID/Pioneer Square pg. 19-24
8. Columbia City pg. 24-26
9. Deldridge pg. 26-28
10. Downtown Commercial Core pg. 28-31
11. Duwamish/ SODO pg. 31-34
12. First Hill pg. 34-37
13. Georgetown pg. 38-40
14. Greenlake pg. 40-42
15. Greenwood/Phinney Ridge pg. 43-44
16. Highland Park pg. 45-46
17. Interbay pg. 46-47
18. Judkins Park pg. 47-48
19. Lake City pg. 48-50
20. Mt. Baker/North Rainier pg. 51-54
21. Northgate pg. 55-56
22. Othello pg. 57-58
23. Queen Anne pg. 58-60
24. Rainier Beach pg. 60-62
25. Ravenna/Bryant pg. 62-64
26. Roxhill/Westwood pg. 64-65
27. Seward Park pg. 65-66

WANDERING SEATTLE: A CULTURE ODYSSEY

28. South Lake/Denny Triangle pg. 66-70
29. South Park pg. 71-72
30. University District pg. 73-74
31. Wallingford pg. 75-76
32. Wedgewood/ View Ridge pg. 76-78
33. West Seattle Junction/Genesee Hill pg. 78-79
34. References pg. 80
35. Neighborhood Map pg. 81
36. About the Author pg. 82

1. BALLARD

Ballard is an energetic neighborhood in the northwestern part of Seattle, known for its maritime history, Scandinavian heritage, and cultural scene. The primary zip code is 98107, but some parts of the neighborhood also fall under 98117 and 98119. Ballard has an estimated population of about 47,000 residents and land area is approximately 3.61 square miles. The Ballard neighborhood in King County has many young professionals, families, and older adults, with a median age between 35 and 40. Ballard is generally considered a middle to upper-middle-class neighborhood, with the median household income higher than the Seattle average.

ATTRACTIONS

Ballard Locks (Hiram M. Chittenden Locks)
3015 NW 54th St, Seattle, WA 98107
Golden Gardens Park
8498 Seaview Pl NW, Seattle, WA 98108
Ballard Farmer's Market
22nd Ave NW & NW Market St, Seattle, WA 98107
Ballard Historic District
Ballard Ave NW between 22nd Ave NW and 24th Ave NW, Seattle, WA 98107,
Museum of Pop Culture (MoPOP)
325 5th Ave N, Seattle, WA 98109
Ballard Civic Center Park
6020 24th Ave NW, Seattle, WA 98107
The Ballard Library
5614 22nd Ave NW, Seattle, WA 98107
Salmon Bay Park

WANDERING SEATTLE: A CULTURE ODYSSEY

2000 NW 54th St, Seattle, WA 98107

PUBLIC TRANSIT

There are a lot of options for moving around the neighborhood, such as bus routes and bikeshare.

Bus Route:

Ballard is served by the King County Metro buses with buses connecting the neighborhood to downtown Seattle. The bus routes are Rapid Ride D line, which service downtown Seattle routes 17, route 40 and route 44.

Bikeshare:

There are various bikeshare programs like Lime, JUMP (by Uber) and Spin all of which can be accessed through their mobile application service.

FOOD CUISINE

The Walrus and Carpenter
4743 Ballard Ave NW, Seattle, WA 98107
Bergen Place
5420 22nd Ave NW, Seattle, WA 98107
Ray's Boathouse
6049 Seaview Ave NW, Seattle, WA 98107
Ballard Annex Oyster House
5410 Ballard Ave NW, Seattle, WA 98107
Stone burner
5214 Ballard Ave NW, Seattle, WA 98107
Ballard Pizza Company
5107 Ballard Ave NW, Seattle, WA 98107
Skillet Diner
2034 NW 56th, Seattle, WA 98107
Ballard Coffee Works

2060 NW Market St, Seattle, WA 98107
Ballard Beer Company
2050 NW Market St, Seattle, WA 98107
Ballard Farmer's Market

Vernon Place NW and 22nd Ave NW, Seattle, WA 98107

2. BEACON HILL

Beacon Hill neighborhood is a community where immigrants from all over the globe have settled together for over a century, located in the southeast of downtown with a rich history, diversity and sweeping views of the city and surrounding mountains. It offers a blend of commercial and green spaces. Beacon Hill has a population of around 40,000 residents. The neighborhood has a moderate population density, which includes both single-family homes, mid density apartments and town houses contributing to a buzzing atmosphere. The Beacon Hill, located in King County, its zip code is 98144, although some parts of the neighborhood fall under 98108 and 98118. The land area of Beacon Hill neighborhood is 7.25 square miles.

ATTRACTIONS
Jefferson Park
3801 Beacon Ave S, Seattle, WA 98144
Washington State Convention Center
800 Convention Pl, Seattle, WA 98101
The Beacon Food Forest
Beacon Ave S & S Spokane St, Seattle, WA 98144
Dr. Jose Rizal Park
1008 12th Ave S, Seattle, WA 98144

Pacific Science Center
200 2nd Ave N, Seattle, WA 98109
Beacon Hill Library
2821 Beacon Ave S, Seattle, WA 98144
Hing Hay Park
423 Maynard Ave S, Seattle, WA 98104

PUBLIC TRANSIT

Light Rail:

The Beacon Hill station is part of the Transit Links light rail station which connects Beacon Hill to downtown Seattle, University of Washington, and Seattle-Tacoma International Airport.

Bus Routes:

King County Metro operates **bus routes 36, 60 and 107**, which make connections at Othello station, West Seattle, Capitol Hill, Renton, Skyway and Rainier Beach.

Bikeshare:

There are various bikeshare programs like Lime, JUMP (by Uber) and Spin all of which can be accessed through their mobile application service.

FOOD CUISINE

Inay's Asian Pacific Cuisine
2503 Beacon Ave S, Seattle, WA 98144

Musang
2524 Beacon Ave S, Seattle, WA 98144

Oriental Mart
1506 S Jackson St, Seattle, WA 98144
Bar del Corso
3507 Beacon Ave S, Seattle, WA 98144
Homer
3013 Beacon Ave S, Seattle, WA 98144

Perihelion Brewery
2800 S Hanford St, Seattle, WA 98144
Tippe and Drague Alehouse
3315 Beacon Ave S, Seattle, WA 98144
Coffeeaholic House
3128 Beacon Ave S, Seattle, WA 98144
Milk Drunk
2805 Beacon Ave S, Seattle, WA 98144
The Station
2533 16th Ave S, Seattle, WA 98144
Baja Bistro
2414 Beacon Ave S, Seattle, WA 98144

3. BELLTOWN

Belltown is a densely populated neighborhood north west of Seattle, Washington. Formerly an artsy, industrial district, in recent times has transformed into a neighborhood of restaurants, boutiques, night clubs and residential towers and art galleries. It's located west of the Denny Triangle neighborhood and in close proximity to the Amazon headquarters and the Cornish College of Arts. The Belltown is in King County, its zip code is 98121 has a land mass of 0.56 square miles, a population of 13,000 residents.

WANDERING SEATTLE: A CULTURE ODYSSEY

ATTRACTIONS

Olympic Sculpture Park
2901 Western Ave, Seattle, WA 98121

The Crocodile
2200 2nd Ave, Seattle, WA 98121

Cinerama
2100 4th Ave, Seattle, WA 98121

Belltown P-Patch
2000 1st Ave, Seattle, WA 98121

Bell Street Park
2001 Bell St, Seattle, WA 98121

PUBLIC TRANSIT

Bus Routes

The bus RapidRide D Line travels along 3rd Avenue with Route 1, Route 2, Route 13 and Route 29 which are the main bus lines that connect Belltown to downtown.

Streetcar

Also, the South Lake Union Streetcar line runs from downtown to South Lake Union with stops in Belltown such as Westlake Ave & Denny Way, Westlake Ave & Thomas St, Westlake Ave & Harrison St.

Bike and Pedestrian Path

Belltown neighborhood due to its strategic location to downtown is about 15-20 mins by walking depending on your location.

Bikeshare:

There are few bikeshare programs like Lime, Veoride which can be accessed through their mobile application service.

Elliott Trail is a popular scenic run along the waterfront connecting Belltown to attractions like the Olympic Sculpture Park and the Seattle Waterfront.

Bell Street Park Trail is an urban oasis located in Bell Street that runs through the heart of Belltown providing greenspace with pedestrian pathways for long walks.

FOOD CUISINE

The 5 Point Café
415 Cedar St, Seattle WA 98119
Shaker + Spear
2000 2nd Ave, Seattle, WA 98121
Japonessa Sushi Cocina
1400 1st Ave, Seattle, WA 98101
Assaggio Ristorante
2010 4th Ave, Seattle, WA 98121
Petra Mediterranean Bistro
2501 4th Ave, Seattle, WA 98121
Le Pichet
1933 1st Ave, Seattle, WA 98101**, Taqueria Cantina** 3130 Western Ave, Seattle, WA 98121,

Bounty Kitchen 801 Vine St, Seattle, WA 98121, **Street Bean Coffee Roasters** 2711 3rd Ave, Seattle, WA 98121.

4. BROADVIEW/ BITTERLAKE

Broadview neighborhood got its name because of the panoramic views of Puget Sound. Located on the Northwest side of Seattle, in the King County region. Broadview neighborhood has a land area of 1.25 square miles, population of 7,200 and the zip code is 98177.

Bitter Lake neighborhood is east of Puget Sound, and named after its most characteristic feature Bitter Lake. It was mostly a forest rich in lumber such as Douglas fir and western Redcedar, inhabited by Native Americans until the late 19th century. The Bitter Lake neighborhood is located in King County, home to 15,000 residents, with a land mass of 1.4 square miles. The zip code for the neighborhood is 98133.

ATTRACTIONS
Broadview Public Library
12755 Greenwood Ave N, Seattle, WA 98133
Broadview Community Church
450 NE 125th St, Seattle, WA 98125

PUBLIC TRANSIT
Bus Routes
The **King County Metro** have bus routes that serve the Broadview neighborhood some major routes are Route 5, Route 28 and Route 40

Bitter Lake also is serviced by the King County Metro connecting residents through various parts of Seattle. The major bus routes are Route 5, Route 28, Route 345 and Route 346

Light Rail
There is a light system which operates from the **Northgate Station** close to Broadview. It connects downtown Seattle to

University of Washington amongst other destinations. Bitter Lake also makes use of the close proximity of Northgate Station to access the Light Rail services.

Park-and-Ride

The **Northgate Station** is also popular with Park-and-Ride service. For some residents who wish to drive to the station and board the public transit. This is often used by both Broadview and Bitter Lake residents.

Bikeshare

There are a few bikeshare programs like Lime and Spin which can be accessed through their mobile application service.

FOOD CUISINE

Lenny's Good Sandwiches
10406 Greenwood Ave N, Seattle, WA 98133
Twin Gardens
11101 Greenwood Ave N, Seattle, WA 98133
Pho Tic Tac
10007 Aurora Ave N, Seattle, WA 98133
Teriyaki Bowl
14330 Greenwood Ave N, Seattle, WA 98133
Los Chilangos
11728 Aurora Ave N, Seattle, WA 98133
Padrino's Pizza
14324 Greenwood Ave N, Seattle, WA 98133
Gyro Stop
13201 Aurora Ave N, Seattle, WA 98133
Broadview Tap House
10004 Greenwood Ave N, Seattle, WA 98133
Asian Wok

WANDERING SEATTLE: A CULTURE ODYSSEY

12233 Aurora Ave N, Seattle, WA 98133
Bitter Lake
8202 Greenwood Ave N, Seattle, WA 98133
Burgermaster
9820 Aurora Ave N, Seattle WA 98103
Thai Chulengos Kitchen
14319 Greenwood Ave N, Seattle WA 98133,
El Naranjo
10002 Aurora Ave N, Seattle, WA 98133
Adulis Eritrean and Ethiopian Restaurant
10515 Greenwood Ave N, Seattle, WA 98133

5. CAPITOL HILL

Capitol Hill located to the east of Seattle in King County is a densely populated neighborhood with a scenic view of Lake Union. Founded by James A. Moore during February 4, 1886 annexation to Seattle. Capitol Hill has a land area of 1.64 square miles, population of 32,144. Today is a vibrant neighborhood with a trendy night life. Capitol Hill has a rich musical heritage and is often known as the birthplace of grunge music made popular by rock band Nirvana in the 1990's. The zip code for Capitol Hill is 98102, 98112 and 98122.

ATTRACTIONS

Volunteer Park
1247 15th Ave E, Seattle WA 98112

Cal Anderson Park
1635 11th Ave, Seattle, WA 98122

Elliott Bay Book Company
1521 10th Ave, Seattle WA 98122

Seattle Asian Art Museum
1400 E Prospect St, Seattle, WA 98112

Melrose Market
1531 Melrose Ave, Seattle, WA 98122

Seattle Central College Arboretum
1701 Broadway, Seattle, WA 98122

The Capitol Hill Murals with various locations around the neighborhood features colorful and unique murals wrapped around buildings embracing local artistic talent.

PUBLIC TRANSIT

Bus Routes

WANDERING SEATTLE: A CULTURE ODYSSEY

The King County Metro Bus operates bus routes providing connections to various parts of Seattle and surrounding neighborhoods. The Route 10, Route 11, Route 43, Route 49 and Route 60 all make connections through Capitol Hill to downtown Seattle.

Light Rail
This station is located 140 Broadway E, Seattle, WA 98102 at Broadway and E Denny Way, which is a hub for the Link Light Rail System, providing an easy access to downtown Seattle, the Sea-Tac Airport and University of Washington.

Street Car
The First Hill Line located at 121 Broadway, Seattle, WA 98102 connects Capitol Hill through Broadway and Denny to the International District, First Hill and Pioneer Square.

Bikeshare
There are a few bikeshare programs like Lime and Spin all of which can be accessed through their mobile application service.

Pedestrian-Friendly
Capitol Hill is very pedestrian friendly with many attractions like shops and attraction within walking distance.

Park-and-Ride
There are facilities for Park-and-Ride located in transit hubs like the University of Washington Station and Northgate Station.

FOOD CUISINE
Skillet Diner
1400 E Union St, Seattle, WA 98122
Oddfellows Café + Bar
1525 10th Ave, Seattle, WA 98122

Momiji
1522 12th Ave, Seattle, WA 98122
Tamarind Tree
501 Terry Ave N, Seattle, WA 98109
Ramen Danbo
1222 E Pine St, Seattle, WA 98122
Mezcaleria Oaxaca
422 E Pine St, Seattle, WA 98122
Tacos Chukis
219 Broadway E, Seattle, WA 98102
Ristorante Machiavelli
1215 Pine St, Seattle, WA 98101
Via Tribunali
913 E Pike St, Seattle, WA 98122
Omega Ouzeri
1529 14th Ave, Seattle, WA 98122
Bakery Nouveau
137 15th Ave E, Seattle, WA 98112
General Porpoise Doughnuts
1020 E Union St, Seattle, WA 98122, **Unicorn**
1118 E Pike St, Seattle, WA 98122
Poppy
622 Broadway E, Seattle, WA 98102.

6. CENTRAL AREA

The Central District is a multicultural residential cluster of historically African American neighborhoods. The Central District is located in King County on the east of Seattle, has strong ties to jazz music, civil rights movements and vibrant cultural traditions. The Population of Central District is 29,868, a land area of 1.64 square miles, and the zip code is 98122.

ATTRACTIONS

Northwest African American Museum
2300 S Massachusetts St, Seattle, WA 98144
Langston Hughes Performing Arts Institute
104 17th Ave S, Seattle, WA 98144
Pratt Fine Arts Center
1902 S Main St, Seattle, WA 98144
Jimi Hendrix Park
2400 S Massachusetts St, Seattle, WA 98144
Dr. Blanche Lavizzo Park
2100 Jackson St, Seattle, WA 98144
Seattle University
901 12th Ave, Seattle WA 98122
Central Cinema
1411 21st Ave, Seattle, WA 98122
Douglass-Truth Library
2300 E Yesler Way, Seattle, WA 98122
Cheasty Greenspace
2539 24th Ave S, Seattle, WA 98144

PUBLIC TRANSIT

Light Rail

There are nearby stations to the central area which serve the neighborhood such as;

Capitol Hill Station located north connects the downtown Seattle, University of Washington and Sea-Tac airport and

Judkins Park Station connects Central Area to Bellevue, Redmond and other Eastside locations.

Bus Routes

The Central Area is covered by King County Metro Bus Service with bus routes 2, 3, 4, 8, 27 and 48 serving the central area neighborhood and connects to downtown Seattle.

Streetcar

The First Hill streetcar makes connections from Pioneer Square to Capitol Hill through Yesler Terrace, International District/Chinatown and First Hill

Pedestrian Friendly

Central Area is pedestrian friendly with well-maintained sidewalks, crosswalks and pedestrian friendly intersections which contributes to a safe walking environment.

Bikeshare

There are a few bikeshare programs like Lime and Spin all of which can be accessed through their mobile application service.

FOOD CUISINE

Ezell's Famous Chicken
501 23rd Ave, Seattle, WA 98122
Meskel Ethiopian Restaurant
2605 E Cherry St, Seattle, WA 98122
Ras Dashen
2801 E Yesler Way, Seattle WA 98122
Pho Bac
1240 S Jackson St, Seattle, WA 98144
Catfish Corner Express
2213 E Union St, Seattle WA 98122
That Brown Girl Cooks

2008 E Union St, Seattle, WA 98122
Broadcast Coffee
1918 E Yesler Way, Seattle, WA 98122
Lowrider Baking Company
2407 E Union St, Seattle WA 98122
Carnitas Michoacan
7133 Martin Luther King Jr Way S, Seattle, WA 98118
Café Salem
2715 E Cherry St, Seattle, WA 98122
Central Pizza
2901 S Jackson St, Seattle, WA 98144
Chuck's Hop Shop
2001 E Union St, Seattle WA 98122

7. CHINATOWN INTERNATIONAL DISTRICT/PIONEER SQUARE

The Chinatown International District is a thriving neighborhood for the Seattle International community. The Chinatown International District is one of the oldest neighborhoods in the city with a popular history of migration from mostly Asian countries. CID is located in King County, with a population of 6,500 residents, a land area of 0.36 square miles. The zip code associated with this neighborhood is 98101 and 98144.

Pioneer Square

JORDAN BREED

The Pioneer Square neighborhood often known as the "birth place" of Seattle is located in the southwest corner of Downtown Seattle. The neighborhood is known for its renaissance revival architecture, First Thursday art walks and lunch spots. The Pioneer Square population is about 3,000 residents, a land area of 0.34 square miles and zip code is 98104.

ATTRACTIONS

International District/Chinatown Station
5th Avenue S & S Jackson St, Seattle WA 98104
Hing Hay Park
423 Maynard Ave S, Seattle, WA 98104
Wing Luke Museum of the Asian Pacific American Experience
719 S King St, Seattle, WA 98104
Uwajimaya Asian Grocery Store
600 5th Ave S, Seattle, WA 98104
Seattle Pinball Museum
508 Maynard Ave S, Seattle, WA 98104
Danny Woo Community Garden
620 S Main St, Seattle, WA 98104
Kobe Terrace Park
221 6th Ave S, Seattle WA 98104
Chinatown Gate
Intersection of S King St and 5th Ave S, Seattle, WA 98104
Tai Tung Restaurant
655 S King St, Seattle, WA 98104
East/West Bookshop
650 S Orcas St, Seattle, WA 98108.
Pioneer Square Park
100 Yesler Way, Seattle, WA 98104

WANDERING SEATTLE: A CULTURE ODYSSEY

Smith Tower
506 2nd Ave, Seattle, WA 98104
Underground Tour
614 1st Ave, Seattle, WA 98104
Occidental Park
117 S Washington St, Seattle, WA 98104
Klondike Gold Rush National Historical Park
319 2nd Ave S, Seattle, WA 98104
Waterfall Garden Park
219 2nd Ave S, Seattle, WA 98104
King Street Station
303 S Jackson St, Seattle WA 98104
Pioneer Building
600 1st Ave, Seattle, WA 98104
Seattle Mystery Bookshop
117 Cherry St, Seattle WA 98104
Grand Central Bakery and Arcade
214 1st Ave S, Seattle, WA 98104
Milepost
31 211 1st Ave S Seattle, WA 98104

PUBLIC TRANSIT
Bus Routes

King County Metro bus transit serve the CID neighborhood making connections through various neighborhoods in Seattle and buses stopping at key locations as Jackson St, 4th Ave S. CID has the bus route 7, route 36, route70, route 124, route 106 and route 550. Pioneer Square is served by King County Metro bus with various locations throughout the city. Pioneer has bus route 21, route 37, route 41, route 116, route 118, route 120 and route 124.

Light Rail

The CID is served by International District/Chinatown Station and is part of the Seattle's Link Light Rail System operated by Sound Transit. The Link Light Rail connects the CID to Downtown Seattle with notable connections such as University of Washington, Sea-Tac Airport and Capitol Hill. Pioneer Square is served by Pioneer Station on Seattle's Link Light Rail System with connections to Capitol Hill, University of Washington, Sea-Tac Airport and Downtown Seattle.

Streetcar

The First Hill Line connects Capitol Hill to CID and Pioneer Square providing a reliable transit option for residents and tourists.

First Hill Line passes through Pioneer Square providing a convenient connection to Capitol Hill and the Chinatown International District. The stops are

Sounder Commuter Rail

The Pioneer Square is served by the King Street Station which serves as a hub for Sounder Commuter Rail Services. During peak hours their key stops are Pierce, King and Snohomish counties.

Bikeshare

The Chinatown International District and Pioneer Square have the bikeshare programs like Lime, JUMP (by Uber), LimePod and Pronto Cycle Share which can all be accessed through their mobile application service.

FOOD CUISINE

WANDERING SEATTLE: A CULTURE ODYSSEY

Tai Tung
655 S King St, Seattle, WA 98104
Fort St. George
601 S King St, Seattle WA 98104
Tsukushinbo
515 S Main St, Seattle, WA 98104
Hokkaido Ramen Santouka
103 Bellevue Ave E, Seattle, WA 98102
Phnom Penh Noodle House
660 S King St, Seattle, WA 98104
Green Leaf Vietnamese Restaurant
418 8th Ave S, Seattle, WA 98104
Fuji Bakery
526 S King St, Seattle, WA, 98104
Mike's Noodle House
418 Maynard Ave S, Seattle, WA 98104
World Pizza
672 S King St, Seattle, WA 98104
Uwajimaya Food Court
600 5th Ave S, Seattle WA 98104
II Corvo Pasta
217 James St, Seattle, WA 98104
Salumi Artisan Cured Meats
309 3rd Ave S, Seattle, WA 98104
Casco Antiguo
115 Occidental Ave S, Seattle, WA 98104
The London Plane
300 Occidental Ave S, Seattle, WA 98104
Tat's Delicatessen
159 Yesler Way, Seattle, WA 98104

Elysian Fields
542 1st Ave S, Seattle, WA 98104
Good Bar
240 2nd Ave S, Seattle, WA 98104
The Central Saloon
207 1st Ave S, Seattle, WA 98104
Cow Chip Cookies
1501 Western Ave, Seattle, WA 98101
Cantina de San Patricio
1914 Occidental Ave S, Seattle, WA 98101

8. COLUMBIA CITY

Columbia City is a neighborhood that has a small town feel with a metro culture located in the Southeast of Seattle. The neighborhood is known for its friendly and welcoming atmosphere while also been vibrant, diverse and historically rich. Columbia City population is about 13,000 residents, the land area is 1.26 square miles and the zip code is 98118.

ATTRACTIONS

Columbia City Theater
4916 Rainier Ave S, Seattle, WA 98118
Columbia Park
4721 Rainier Ave S, Seattle, WA 98118
Ark Lodge Cinemas
4816 Rainier Ave S, Seattle WA 98118
Columbia City Farmers Market
3700 S Edmunds St, Seattle WA 98118
Genesee Park and Playfield
4316 S Genesee St, Seattle WA 98118
Columbia City Gallery

WANDERING SEATTLE: A CULTURE ODYSSEY

4864 Rainier Ave S, Seattle, WA 98118

PUBLIC TRANSIT

Light Rail

Columbia City Station through the Link Light Rail provides accessibility to the north and south of Seattle with connections to downtown Seattle, University of Washington and Seattle-Tacoma International Airport.

Bus Routes

The King County Metro provides frequent route services through the neighborhood such as route 7, route 50 and route 106.

Pedestrian Paths

Chief Sealth Trail provides a scenic route for cyclists and pedestrians, jogging from Beacon Hill to Rainier Beach.

Bikeshare

There are a few bike share programs in Columbia City neighborhood which are Lime, LINK by Super pedestrian and Spin. All can be located and accessed through their individual mobile application service.

FOOD CUISINE

Wabi-Sabi
4909 Rainier Ave S, Seattle, WA 98118
Tutta Bella Neapolitan Pizzeria
4918 Rainier Ave S, Seattle, WA 98118
The Royal Room
5000 Rainier Ave S, Seattle, WA 98118
Lottie's Lounge
4900 Rainier Ave S, Seattle, WA 98118
Island Soul

4869 Rainier Ave S, Seattle, WA 98118

Geraldine's Counter

4872 Rainier Ave S, Seattle, WA 98118

La Medusa

4857 Rainier Ave S, Seattle, WA 98118

Super Six

3714 S Hudson St, Seattle, WA 98118

Columbia City Bakery 4865 Rainier Ave S, Seattle, WA 98118

Bang Tutte Kitchen 4800 Rainier Ave S, Seattle WA 98118

9. DELDRIDGE

The Deldridge neighborhood is located in West Seattle with a rich history in its natural landscape. The early settlers were the Duwamish residents who lived along the Duwamish River and today the neighborhood is Seattle's most vibrant and diverse community with green spaces and ongoing development. Deldridge neighborhood has an estimated population of 27,271 residents, the land area is 5.72 square miles (city-data.com) and the zip code is 98106, 98108 and 98126.

ATTRACTIONS

Westcrest Park

9000 8th Ave SW, Seattle, WA 98106

Deldridge Playfield

WANDERING SEATTLE: A CULTURE ODYSSEY

4458 Deldridge Way SW, Seattle, WA 98106

Youngstown Cultural Arts Center
4408 Deldridge Way SW, Seattle WA 98106
Camp Long
5200 35th Ave SW, Seattle, WA 98126
Longfellow Creek Trail
28th Ave SW & SW Yancy St, Seattle, WA 98126,
Deldridge Community Center
4501 Deldridge Way SW, Seattle, WA 98106.

PUBLIC TRANSIT
Bus Routes
The King Metro Bus serves the Deldrige neighborhood with routes 120, route 125, route 128 and RapidRide H Line coming soon to replace the route 120.

Bikeshare
There are a few bikeshare programs such as Lime, Spin and Bird. All are accessible via their mobile application service.

FOOD CUISINE
Ounces Tap Room & Beer Garden
3809 Deldridge Way SW, Seattle, WA 98106
Pho Aroma
5605 Deldridge Way SW, Seattle, WA 98106
Nueva Alaskay Restaurant
9413 Deldridge Way SW, Seattle, WA 98106
Tommy's Thai Food
9818 Deldridge Way SW, Seattle, WA 98106
Youngstown Coffee
5210, Deldridge Way SW, Seattle, WA 98106

10. DOWNTOWN COMMERCIAL CORE

Downtown is the central business district of Seattle which is made up of commercial businesses and nightlife. The Downtown Commercial Core is located in King County, boasts a population of 98,000 and growing, a land area of 4 square miles and covered by zip codes 98101, 98104 and 98121. The early settlers Arthur Denny, Carson Boren and William Bell first arrived Alki Point in 1851 and migrated to eastern shore of Elliott Bay with early development of what became Seattle today. A few notable mentions that have shaped the history and landscape of Downtown Seattle Commercial corridor are the **Great Seattle Fire (1889), World's Fair (1962) and Tech Boom (1990s-2000s).**

ATTRACTIONS

Pike Place Market
85 Pike Street, Seattle WA 98101

Seattle Art Museum (SAM)
1300 1st Avenue, Seattle, WA 98101

Seattle Aquarium
1483 Alaskan Way, Pier 59, Seattle, WA 98101

Seattle Great Wheel
1301 Alaskan Way, Seattle WA 98101

Pioneer Square
Yesler Way, 4th Avenue, S King Street, and Alaskan Way, Seattle, WA 98104

The Seattle Waterfront
Alaskan Way between Pier 50 and Pier 70, Seattle, WA 98101

Seattle Central Library
1000 4th Avenue, Seattle, WA 98104
Westlake Center
400 Pine Street, Seattle, WA 98101
Benaroya Hall
200 University Street, Seattle, WA 98101
Sky View Observatory (Columbia Center)
700 4th Avenue, Seattle, WA 98104
The Gum Wall
1428 Post Alley, Seattle, WA 98101 (Near Pike Place Market).

PUBLIC TRANSIT

Bus Routes: The King Country Metro bus services downtown core through bus routes are route 8, route 40, route 62, route 7, route 14, route 49, route 55, route 50, route 545.

Rapid Ride: Also serviced by King County Metro transit is a high-speed bus with a dedicated lane and fewer stops The Rapid Lines are covered by C, D, E.

Link Light Rail is served by Sound Transit and passes through University of Washington, Downtown core, Sea-Tac Airport and Angie Lake.

Sounder Commuter Rail: services Everett and Lakewood to King Street Station in Downtown Seattle.

Streetcar

South Lake Union Line connects Downtown with South Lake Union neighborhood.

First Hill Line connects Capitol Hill, First Hill and the International District/Chinatown to Pioneer Square and the Central Business District.

Monorail

The Monorail Car 1 (Red Train) and Monorail Car 2 (Blue Train) connects West Lake Center Station 400 Pine Street, Seattle, WA 98101 in downtown to Seattle (West Lake Center Mall), to Seattle Center Station 305 Harrison Street, Seattle, WA 98109 (Space Needle).

Ferry

The Washington State Ferry departs downtown ferry terminal (Colman Dock) Pier 52 to Bainbridge Island Ferry Terminal, 270 Olympic Drive SE, **Bainbridge Island**, WA 98110 and Bremerton Ferry Terminal, 211 Pacific Avenue, **Bremerton**, WA 98337. The ferry boat names are MV Wenatchee, MV Tacoma, MV Puyallup, MV Spokane, MV Kitsap, MV Chelan, MV Issaquah.

Water Taxi

The King County Water Taxi provides water service from **Downtown Seattle** Pier 50 Seattle Ferry Terminal to Seacrest Park, 1660 Harbor Avenue SW **West Seattle**, and Vashon Island Ferry Terminal, 10800 North Vashon Highway SW, **Vashon Island**, WA 98070. The water taxi names are Doc Maynard and Sally Fox.

Pedestrian

Walking downtown is safe, enjoyable and pedestrian friendly with many attractions within walking distance.

Bikeshare

There are few services like **Lime, JUMP (by Uber) Spin, Lyft Bikes, Donkey Republic and Zagster** which offer bike rentals through their mobile application service. Also, there is an extensive network of bike lanes and paths throughout downtown.

FOOD CUISINE
The Pink Door
1919 Post Alley, Seattle, WA 98101
Matt's in the Market
94 Pike Street, Seattle, WA 98101
Dahlia Lounge
2001 4th Avenue, Seattle, WA 98121
Taylor Shellfish Oyster Bar
1521 Melrose Avenue, Seattle, WA 98101
Serious Pie
316 Virginia Street, Seattle, WA 98101
II Bistro
93 Pike Street, Seattle, WA 98101
Chan Seattle
86 Pine Street, Seattle, WA 98101
Lola
2000 4th Avenue, Seattle, WA 98121
Sushi Kashiba
86 Pine Street, Suite 1, Seattle, WA 98101
Cutters Crabhouse
2001 Western Avenue, Seattle, WA 98121

11. DUWAMISH/ SODO

Duwamish is a neighborhood located in King County, making up the majority of the city's industrial district. The

Duwamish neighborhood has a population of Duwamish named after the Duwamish River and the indigenous residents who once inhabited the area.

SODO or South of Downtown is in King County, about 4 square miles, has an approximate population of 3,000 residents, zip code in the area is 98134. After the early settlers in the 19th and 20th century, Seattle experienced massive industrialization and growth downtown due to their proximity to manufacturing plants, rail roads and waterfront.

ATTRACTIONS

Duwamish Longhouse and Cultural Center
4705 W Marginal Way SW, Seattle WA 98106
Boeing Plant
8000 E Marginal Way S, Seattle WA 98108
South Park Bridge connects South Park neighborhood to Georgetown
Herring's House Park
7800 Detroit Ave SW, Seattle, WA 98106
Duwamish Waterway Park
7900 10th Ave S, Seattle, WA 98108
Lumen Field (formerly CenturyLink Field)
800 Occidental Ave S, Seattle, WA 98134,
T Mobile Park
1250 1st Ave S, Seattle, WA 98134,
SODO Urbanworks
3901 1st Ave S, Seattle, WA 98134,
The SODO Flea Market
5701 6th Ave S, Seattle, WA 98108,
SODO Track adjacent to the SODO Busway, along 5th Avenue S and 6th Avenue S.

WANDERING SEATTLE: A CULTURE ODYSSEY

PUBLIC TRANSIT
Bus Routes
The King County Metro Transit bus routes are route 21, route 50, route 60, route 132, route 60X (Express).
Bikeshare
There are a few bikeshare programs like Lime, Spin, Bird, Lyft and Uber and are accessible through their mobile application service.
Pedestrian Path
The Duwamish/SODO neighborhood is very pedestrian friendly with sidewalks and crosswalks.
Light Rail
Stadium Station and International District/Chinatown Station as a hub for the Red Line and Blue Line.
Ferry
Washington State Ferries (WSF), King County Water Taxi (West Seattle to Downtown Seattle), Seattle Ferry Terminal at Colman Dock

FOOD CUISINE
SODO Kitchen
3320 1st Ave S, Seattle, WA 98134
Jack's BBQ
3924 Airport Way S, Seattle, WA 98108
Salumi Cured Meats
404 Occidental Ave S, Seattle, WA 98104
Juno
2635 6th Ave S, Seattle, WA 98134
Loretta's Northwesterner
8617 14th Ave S, Seattle, WA 98108

Tacos Chukis
219 Broadway E, Seattle, WA 98102
Pecos Pit Bar-B-Que
2260 1st Ave S, Seattle, WA 98134
Café Con Leche
2901 1st Ave S, Seattle, WA 98134
Columbia City Bakery
3334A Rainier Ave S, Seattle, WA 98144
SODO Deli
3328 1st Ave S, Seattle, WA 98134
Smarty Pants Garage
6017 Airport Way S, Seattle, WA 98108

12. FIRST HILL

The First Hill neighborhood is located in Northwest Seattle, with a land area of 2,100 square miles, a population of 12,500 residents with zip codes 98101. First Hill is a vibrant neighborhood, historic and popular for its urban feel through architectural styles from early 20th-century buildings to modern day skyscrapers.

ATTRACTIONS

Frye Art Museum

704 Terry Ave, Seattle, WA 98104

WANDERING SEATTLE: A CULTURE ODYSSEY

St. James Cathedral

804 9th Ave, Seattle, WA 98104

Freeway Park

700 Seneca St, Seattle, WA 98101

Seattle University

901 12th Ave, Seattle, WA 98122

Swedish Medical Center

Cherry Hill Campus 500 17th Ave, Seattle, WA 98122

Harborview Medical Center

325 9th Ave, Seattle, WA 98104, **Stimson-Green Mansion** (Seattle Architectural Foundation) 1204 Minor Ave, Seattle, WA 98101.

PUBLIC TRANSIT

Bus Route: There are buses operated by King County Metro with bus route 2, route 3, route 4, route 12 and route 60 running through First Hill to downtown Seattle.'

Streetcar: This is operated by the First Hill Line running through First Hill, Capitol Hill and Pioneer Square.

Light Rail (Sound Transit Link): There is also the option of the Sound Transit Link which is within walking distance. The Light rail helps to connect the University of Washington to SeaTac Airport.

Bikeshare: The are a few bikeshare programs available like Lime and JUMP (by Uber) and can be accessed through their various mobile application service.

Pedestrian: The First City neighborhood has a walkable street and lots of green space like Freeway Park.

FOOD CUISINE
Cherry Street Coffee House
1212 1st Ave, Seattle, WA 98101
The Carlile Room
820 Pine St, Seattle, WA 98101
Café Presse
1117 12th Ave, Seattle, WA 98122
Cantina Lena
2101 7th Ave, Seattle, WA 98121
Petra Mediterranean Bistro
2501 4th Ave, Seattle, WA 98121
Thai Tom
4543 University Way, NE Seattle, WA 98105
Harbor City Restaurant
707 S King St, Seattle, WA 98104
Starbucks Reserve Roastery
1124 Pike St, Seattle, WA 98101
Mamnoon
1508 Melrose Ave, Seattle, WA 98122

WANDERING SEATTLE: A CULTURE ODYSSEY

Barolo Ristorante
1940 Westlake Ave, Seattle, WA 98101.

13. GEORGETOWN

Georgetown neighborhood is the oldest neighborhood located in the Northwest Seattle. Founded on September 27, 1851 by Luther Collins, Henry Van Asselt and the Maple family. The Georgetown neighborhood is bounded on the North by Greater Duwamish, bounded on the south by Allentown, to the east by Beacon Hill and the west by Deldrige. The population of Georgetown neighborhood is about 2,500 residents, a land area of 2.2 square miles and zip code is 98108.

ATTRACTIONS

Museum of Flight
9404 E Marginal Way S, Seattle, WA 98108
Georgetown Steam Plant
6605 13th Ave S, Seattle, WA 98108
Fantagraphics Bookstore & Gallery
1202 S Vale St, Seattle, WA 98108
Georgetown Trailer Park Mall
5805 Airport Way S, Seattle, WA 98108
Oxbow Park
6430 Corson Ave S, Seattle, WA 98108
The Georgetown Stables
980 S Nebraska St, Seattle, WA 98108
Georgetown Arts and Cultural Center
5809 Airport Way S, Seattle, WA 98108
Georgetown Records
1201 S Vale St #2, Seattle, WA 98108

PUBLIC TRANSIT

WANDERING SEATTLE: A CULTURE ODYSSEY

Bus Route: The King County Metro bus routes that serve Georgetown neighborhood are route 60, route 124, route 131 and route 132.

Light Rail: The nearby SODO station offers an easy access to Georgetown, while providing connections to downtown Seattle, the University of Washington, and SeaTac Airport.

Bikeshare: The are a few bikeshare programs available like Lime and Bird and can be accessed through their various mobile application service.

FOOD CUISINE

The Corson Building
5609 Corson Ave S, Seattle, WA 98108
Chilolos
5963 Corson Ave S, Seattle, WA 98108
Kauai Family Restaurant
6324 6th Ave S, Seattle, WA 98108
Ciudad
6118 12th Ave S, Seattle, WA 98108
Star Brass Lounge
5629 Airport Way S, Seattle, WA 98108
Matcha Man Ice Cream & Taiyaki
6003 12th Ave S, Seattle, WA 98108
Mezzanotte
1210 S Bailey St, Seattle, WA 98108
Hangar Café
6261 13th Ave S, Seattle, WA 98108 **Georgetown Liquor Company**

5501 Airport Way S, Seattle, WA 98108
Fonda La Catrina
5905 Airport Way S, Seattle WA 98108
Deep Sea Sugar & Salt
6601 Carleton Ave S, Seattle, WA 98108

14. GREENLAKE

The neighborhood of Green Lake is in the north central of Seattle, Washington. It is an area recognized for its picturesque Green Lake. The population is about 12,000 residents, the size is 2.8 square miles and the zip codes for the region are 98103 and 98115.

ATTRACTIONS

Green Lake Park

7201 E Green Lake Dr. N, Seattle, WA 98115

Woodland Park Zoo

5500 Phinney Ave N, Seattle, WA 98103

Green Lake Small Craft Center

5900 W Green Lake Way N, Seattle, WA 98103

Green Lake Community Center and Evans Pool

7201 E Green Lake Dr N, Seattle, WA 98115
Seattle Public Theater at Bathhouse
7312 W Green Lake Dr N, Seattle, WA 98103
Green Lake Library
7364 E Green Lake Dr N, Seattle, WA 98115

PUBLIC TRANSIT

Bus Route: The King County Metro operates several bus routes that connect Green Lake with other neighborhoods. The bus routes are route 20, route 26, route 45, route 62.

Light Rail: The proximity to the Northgate Station provides a quick access to downtown Seattle, the University of Washington and other areas.

Park-and-Ride: Northgate station provides parking facilities for commuters who wish to use public transportation into the city.

Bikeshare: The Seattle Free Floating Bikeshare, Lime and Veo all operate dockless bikes in the neighborhood and are available to rent through their various mobile application service.

FOOD CUISINE

Nell's Restaurant
6804 E Green Lake Way N, Seattle, WA 98115
Duke's Sea Food
7850 Green Lake Dr N, Seattle WA, 98103
Tutta Bella Neapolitan Pizzeria
4411 Stone Way N, Seattle, WA 98103
The Shelter Lounge

JORDAN BREED

7110 E Green Lake Dr N, Seattle, WA 98115
Mighty-O Donuts
2110 N 55th St, Seattle, WA 98103
Frelard Tamales
6412 Latona Ave NE, Seattle, WA 98115
Rosita's Mexican Grill
7210 Woodland Ave NE, Seattle, WA 98115
Bongos Café
6501 Aurora Ave N, Seattle, WA 98103

15. GREENWOOD/ PHINNEY RIDGE

The neighborhood of Greenwood is located in the north central Seattle, Washington. The population is approximately 28,000, the land area is 1.5 square miles and zip code is 98103.

The Phinney Ridge neighborhood is located in north central Seattle, adjacent to Greenwood and Ballard. The population is about 8,500 residents, with approximately 1.5 square miles, and zip code is 98103.

ATTRACTIONS
Greenwood Park
602 N 87th St, Seattle, WA 98103
Woodland Park Zoo
5500 Phinney Ave N, Seattle, WA 98103

Greenwood Space Travel Supply Company
841 Greenwood Ave N, Seattle, WA 98103
The Greenwood Collective
8536 Greenwood Ave N, Seattle, WA 98103
Phinney Center
6532 Phinney Ave N, Seattle, WA 98103
Taproot Theatre Company
204 N 85th St, Seattle, WA 98103
Greenwood Car Show (annual event and specific locations vary each year) Phinney Ridge Lutheran Church 7500 Greenwood Ave N, Seattle, WA 98103.

PUBLIC TRANSIT

Bus Route: The Metro County Bus has route 5, route 26, route 28, route 40, route 62.

Light Rail: The closest station is Northgate station which is accessible with bus route 5 and 40.

Bikeshare: There are bike share programs like Lime and JUMP (BY Uber) which are accessible through their mobile application service.

FOOD CUISINE
Kidd Valley
7802 Aurora Ave N, Seattle, WA 98103
Alejandro's Mexican Food
8050 Greenwood Ave N, Seattle, WA 98103
Pho Bac
1245 N 85th St, Seattle, WA 98103
The Oak
2820 NE 55th St, Seattle, WA 98105
Woodland Park Zoo Café
5500 Phinney Ave N, Seattle, WA 98103
The Fat Hen
1414 NW 70th St, Seattle, WA 98103
Taproot Theatre Company Café
204 N 85th St, Seattle, WA 98103
Paseo
6226 Seaview Ave NW, Seattle, WA 98107

16. HIGHLAND PARK

The Highland Park neighborhood is located in the Southwest part of Seattle, Washington. The early development was in early 1900s as part of the broader growth of West Seattle. It attracted settlers due to its affordability and proximity to downtown Seattle. **In 1907, Highland Park was annexed into the city of Seattle**. After World War II Highland Park saw increased residential construction during this period contributing a whole lot to its suburban character. The land area of the Highland Park is 1.2 square miles, the population is about 7,000 residents and the zip code is 98106.

ATTRACTIONS

Highland Park Playground 1100 SW Cloverdale St, Seattle, WA 98106 **Westcrest Park** 9000 8th Ave SW, Seattle, WA 98106

Highland Park Improvement Club (HPIC) 1116 SW Holden St, Seattle, WA 98106

Southwest Branch Library 9010 35th Ave SW, Seattle, WA 98126.

PUBLIC TRANSIT

Bus Route: The King County Metro Bus has several routes which are route 120, route 22, route 21 and route 118.

Bikeshare: There are bike share programs such as Lime and Spin which are easily accessible through their mobile application service.

FOOD CUISINE

Taqueria El Rinconsito
6745 35th Ave SW, Seattle, WA 98126

The Highland Park Bar & Grill
1012 SW Holden St, Seattle, WA 98106
Szechaun Chef
7417 35th Ave, SW Seattle, WA 98126
Aladdin's
6244 35th Ave AW, Seattle, WA 98126
Papa John's Pizza
6019 35th Ave SW, Seattle, WA 98126
Toshi's Teriyaki 6400 35th Ave SW, Seattle, WA 98126.

17. INTERBAY

The neighborhood of Interbay is located at Northwest of Seattle, Washington. It consists of a valley between Queen Anne Hill on the east and Magnolia on the west. The population in Interbay neighborhood is about 2,000 residents, the land area is 1.2 square miles and the zip code is 98109.

ATTRACTIONS

Interbay Golf Center
2501 15th Ave W, Seattle, WA 98199
Elliott Bay Trail access points near 15th Ave W, Seattle, WA 98019
Kinnear Park
201 W Kinnear Pl, Seattle, WA 98109
Queen Anne Bowl
1400 1st Ave W, Seattle, WA 98109
Seattle Pacific University
3307 3rd Ave W, Seattle, WA 98199

PUBLIC TRANSIT

Bus Route: The King County Metro Bus has several routes which are route 19, route 32, route 40.

Bikeshare: There are bike share programs like Lime and Spin which are easily accessible through their mobile application service.

FOOD CUISINE
The Ballard Locks Café
3015 14th Ave W, Seattle, WA 98109
The Interbay Pizza
2416 15th Ave W, Seattle, WA 98199
Noodle Land
4104 15th Ave W, Seattle, WA 98199
Kokyo Teriyaki
1500 W Nickerson St, Seattle, WA 98109

18. JUDKINS PARK

The neighborhood of Judkins Park is located on East of Seattle Washington and known for its green spaces and community atmosphere. The Judkins Park is located between the Central District and Capitol Hill neighborhoods. The population is about 3,000 residents, a land area of 0.9 square miles and zip code is 98144.

ATTRACTIONS
Judkins Park
2150 S Norman St, Seattle, WA 98144
Judkins Park Community Center
2150 S Norman St, Seattle, WA 98144 (located within the park limits)

PUBLIC TRANSIT
Bus Route: The King County Metro Bus Routes operates different routes such as route 4, route 7, route 9.

Light Rail
The closest light rail is the Capital Hill Station located a short distance away. It provides connections between downtown Seattle and University of Washington.

Bikeshare: There are bike share programs such as Lime and Spin which are easily accessible through their mobile application service.

FOOD CUISINE
All notable mentions for food are located in nearby Capitol Hill.

19. LAKE CITY
The neighborhood of Lake City Is located in the Northeast region of Seattle along Lake City Way NE (SR-522) downtown Seattle. The population is approximately 40,000 residents, the land area is 3.8 square miles and the zip code is 98125, 98115 and 98133.

ATTRACTIONS
Lake City Farmers Market
12501 28th Ave NE, Seattle, WA 98125
Albert Davis Park
12526 27th Ave NE, Seattle, WA 98125
Virgil Flaim Park
12336 28th Ave NE, Seattle, WA 98125
The Seattle Public Library Lake City Branch 12501 28th Ave NE, Seattle, WA 98125
Kaffeeklatsch Seattle
12513 Lake City Way NE, Seattle, WA 98125

Elliott Bay Public House & Brewery
12537 Lake City Way NE, Seattle, WA 98125
Lake City Mini Park
12539 Lake City Way NE, Seattle, WA 98125
Thriftway Grocery Store
1026 NE 125th St, Seattle, WA 98125
Lake City Community Center
12531 28th Ave NE, Seattle, WA 98125
Cedar Park
Near NE 135th St and Sand Point Way NE, Seattle, WA 98125
The Lake City Mural
12759 Lake City Way NE, Seattle, WA 98125.

PUBLIC TRANSIT

Bus Route: The King County Metro bus has destinations through the neighborhood such as route 41, route 65, route 75, route 372, route 522.

Light Rail

The closest train station is Northgate station which is accessible through route 41 and 75. This connects Downtown Capitol Hill, and University of Washington.

Park-and-Ride

There are Park-and-Ride services in Northgate station for those commuters who don't want to drive to Downtown and can park their vehicles and commute by public transit.

Bikeshare: There are options for bike share programs such as Lime, Spin and Link which can all be accessed through their various mobile application service.

FOOD CUISINE

Kaffeeklatsch
12513 Lake City Way NE, Seattle, WA 98125
Elliott Bay Public House & Brewery
12537 Lake City Way NE, Seattle, WA 98125
Toyoda Sushi
12543 Lake City Way NE, Seattle, WA 98125
Los Pepitos Locos
12336 Lake City Way, NE, Seattle, WA 98125
Pho An
12508 Lake City Way NE, Seattle, WA 98125
Heaven Sent Fried Chicken
14330 Lake City Way NE, Seattle, WA 98125
Amante Pizza and Pasta
12319 Roosevelt Way NE, Seattle, WA 98125
Thai One
12526 Lake City Way NE, Seattle, WA 98125
Lake City Gyros
12325 Lake City Way NE, Seattle, WA 98125
Moroccan Flavors
12525 Lake City Way NE, Seattle, WA 98125

20. MT. BAKER/ NORTH RAINIER

Mount Baker is a vibrant and historic neighborhood located in southeast of Seattle. Popularly known for its scenic views of Lake Washington and the Cascade mountains. The population of Mount Baker is approximately 10,000 residents, the land area is 1.84 square miles and the zip code is 98144.

North Rainier is a neighborhood in southeast Seattle, in close proximity to Mount Baker neighborhood. The population is approximately 5,000 residents, the land area is 0.92 square miles and zip code is 98144.

ATTRACTIONS

Mount Baker Park
2521 Lake Park Dr S, Seattle, WA 98144

Mount Baker Beach
2301 Lake Washington Blvd S, Seattle, WA 98144

Coleman Park
1526 Lake Washington Blvd S, Seattle, WA 98144

Cheasty Greenspace
2530 S Grand St, Seattle, WA 98144

Mount Baker Community Club
2811 Mount Rainier Dr S, Seattle WA 98144

Franklin High School
3013 S Mount Baker Blvd, Seattle WA 98144

Sam Smith Park
1400 Martin Luther King Jr Way S, Seattle, WA 98144

Judkins Park
2150 S Norman St, Seattle, WA 98144

John C. Little Sr. Park

JORDAN BREED

6961 37th Ave S, Seattle, WA 98118

PUBLIC TRANSIT

Bus Route: The King County Metro bus service has routes 7, route 8, route 14 and route 48 providing access to downtown Seattle, Capitol Hill and the central District. For North Rainier bus routes 7, route 9, route 36, route 50 and route 106 take you to downtown Seattle, the International District and Sea Tac Airport.

Light Rail: The station is located at 2700 Martin Luther King Jr Way S, Seattle WA 98144 with connections to downtown Seattle, University of Washington and SeaTac Airport. For North Rainier, the Beacon Hill Station is in close proximity at 27090 Beacon Ave S, Seattle, WA 98144. The station provides access to downtown Seattle, the University of Washington and SeaTac Airport.

Pedestrian Trail: the **I-90 Trail** is a multipurpose trail through Mount Baker community connecting to other trails and green spaces also popularly known for biking, walking and running. Also, there is the **Lake Washington Boulevard** a very popular cycling route with scenic views of the lake. **Mountains to Sound Greenway Trail** another popular biking route and the **Chief Sealth Trail** has connections to the city and also popular among cyclists.

Bikeshare: There is a bike share program like Lime and JUMP (by Uber) and is easily accessible through their various mobile application service.

FOOD CUISINE
The Red Mill Burgers
1600 W Nickerson St, Seattle, WA 98119
Bamboo Garden
4200 S Rainier Ave, Seattle, WA 98118
Himalayan Sherpa Kitchen
1102 34th Ave, Seattle, WA 98122
Thai Tom
4540 University Way NE, Seattle, WA 98105
La Cocina
2918 S Rainier Ave, Seattle, WA 98144
Tacos El Asadero
3215 S, 140th St, Seattle, WA 98168
Chaco Canyon Organic Café
2035 15th Ave S, Seattle, WA 98144
Café Flora
2901 East Madison St, Seattle, WA 98112
Mount Baker Café
2715 Rainier Ave S, Seattle, WA 98144
Columbia City Bakery
4865 Rainier Ave S, Seattle, WA 98118
Rookies Sports Bar
3800 Rainier Ave S, Seattle, WA 98118
Matsu Sushi
4546 Rainier Ave S, Seattle, WA 98118
Pho 15

JORDAN BREED

4242 Rainier Ave S, Seattle, WA 98118
Tai Tung Restaurant
6521 Rainier Ave S, Seattle, WA 98118
Los Chatos Tacos
3914 Rainier Ave S, Seattle, WA 98118
El Chupacabra
1830 S 19th St, Seattle, WA 98144
Vega Haven

6501 4th Ave S, Seattle, WA 98108
Victrola Coffee Roasters
3215 S, 140th St, Seattle, WA 98168
Columbia City Bakery
4865 Rainier Ave S, Seattle WA 98118

21. NORTHGATE

The Northgate neighborhood is located in the northeast region of Seattle. It is bordered by Maple Leaf to the south, Lake City to the north and Roosevelt to the west. The population is approximately 12,000 residents, the land area is about 1.5 square miles and the zip code is 98125.

ATTRACTIONS

Northgate Mall
401 NE Northgate Way, Seattle, WA 98125
Northgate Park
1050 NE 115th St, Seattle, WA 98125
Thornton Creek
Intersection of NE 107th St and 35th Ave NE, WA 98125
Seattle Public Library-Northgate Branch
10548 5th Ave NE, Seattle WA 98125
North Seattle College
9600 College Way N, Seattle, WA 98103
Northgate Ice Arena
10510 5th Ave NE, Seattle, WA 98125

PUBLIC TRANSIT

Bus Route: King County Metro is served by route 40, route 41 with connections to Fremont and Ballard and downtown Seattle.

Light Rail: The Northgate station is a major hub with connections to downtown Seattle and other parts of the city.

Transit Center: This is a central hub for buses providing transfers between different routes.

Bikeshare: There is a bikeshare program such as Lime and Spin which are both accessible through their mobile application service.

FOOD CUISINE:
Kizuki Ramen & Izakaya
319 NE Thornton Pl, Seattle, WA 98125
Thai Fusion Bistro
12310 15th Ave NE, Seattle, WA 98125
Five Guys
401 Northgate Way Suite 470, Seattle WA 98125
The Saffron Grill
2132 N Northgate Way, Seattle, WA 98133
Chipotle
401 NE Northgate Way, Suite 428, Seattle, WA 98125
Gyro House
7702 Aurora Ave N, Seattle, WA 98103
MOD Pizza
401 NE Northgate Way, Suite 475, Seattle, WA 98125
Olive Garden
401 NE Northgate Way, Seattle, WA 98125
Masala of India Cuisine
507 NE Northgate Way, Seattle, WA 98125
Chutneys Bistro
12343 Lake City Way NE, Seattle, WA 98125
Bluefin Sushi & Seafood
401 NE Northgate Way, Suite 430, Seattle, WA 98125
Cold Stone Creamery 401 NE Northgate Way, Suite 428, Seattle, WA 98125

22. OTHELLO

The neighborhood of Othello is a diverse and vibrant neighborhood located in Northwest region of Seattle. The population is approximately 10,000 residents, the land area is 1.5 square miles and zip code is 98118.

ATTRACTIONS:
Othello Park
4351 S Othello St, Seattle WA 98118

PUBLIC TRANSIT
Bus Route:
The King County Metro bus has routes 7, route 9, route 106.

Light Rail: The Othello station is located at **4200 S Othello St** with destinations to downtown Seattle, Sea-Tac Airport and other neighborhoods.

Park-and-Ride: the nearby Park-and-Ride facilities allow commuters to drive and park their vehicles before transferring to public transportation into the city.

Bikeshare: The bikeshare program has options such as Lime and Spin and can be accessed through their various mobile application service.

FOOD CUISINE
Pho Tai
6820 15th Ave S, Seattle, WA 98108
Bananas Grill
6798 15th Ave S, Seattle, WA 98108
The Original Philly's
4451 S Othello St, Seattle, WA 98118

Sweet Alchemy
1010 11th Ave, Seattle, WA 98122

23. QUEEN ANNE

The Queen Anne neighborhood is well known for its charming views, culture and history. It is located northwest of downtown Seattle. The population is about 36,000 residents, the land area is 7.3 square miles and the zip code is 98109 but some parts of the neighborhood are 98119.

ATTRACTIONS

Kerry Park
211 W Highland Dr, Seattle, WA 98119

Seattle Center (includes Space Needle, MoPOP, Chihuly Garden and Glass, Pacific Science Center) 305 Harrison St, Seattle, WA 98109

Queen Anne Avenue
Queen Anne Ave N, Seattle, WA 98109

Myrtle Edwards Park
3130 Alaskan Way, Seattle, WA 98121

Parsons Gardens
650 W Highland Dr, Seattle, WA 98119

Bhy Kracke Park
1215 5th Ave N, Seattle, WA 98109

Kinnear Park
899 W Olympic Pl, Seattle, WA 98119

PUBLIC TRANSIT

Bus Route: The King County Metro bus service has route 2, route 3, route 4, route 13 and RapidRide D Line with connections to various neighborhoods and downtown Seattle.

Monorail: The Seattle Center Station makes connections to Queen Anne to downtown Seattle.

Light Rail: The Westlake Station is the closest light rail station with connections to buses or the monorail.

Streetcar: The South Lake Union Street Car is nearby with connections from South Lake Union to downtown Seattle with transfers to buses or mono rail.

Bikeshare: There is a bikeshare program such as Lime and JUMP (by Uber) with access through their various mobile application service.

FOOD CUISINE

Toulouse Petit Kitchen & Lounge
601 Queen Anne Ave N, Seattle, WA 98109
5 Spot
1502 Queen Anne Ave N, Seattle, WA 98109
How to Cook a Wolf
2208 Queen Anne Ave N, Seattle, WA 98109
Via Tribunali
317 W Galer St, Seattle, WA 98119
Uptown China Restaurant
200 Queen Anne Ave N, Seattle, WA 98109
Shanty Café
350 Elliott Ave W, Seattle, WA 98119
Mezcaleria Oaxaca
2123 Queen Anne Ave N, Seattle, WA 98109
Plaza Garibaldi
129 1st Ave W, Seattle, WA 98119
Taylor Shellfish Farms

124 Republican St, Seattle, WA 98109
Le Reve Bakery
1805 Queen Anne Ave N, Seattle, WA 98109
Bistro Shirlee
2226 Queen Anne Ave N, Seattle, WA 98109
Caffe Ladro
600 Queen Anne Ave N, Seattle, WA 98109
El Diablo Coffee Co.
1825 Queen Anne Ave N, Seattle, WA 98109
Citizen Six
1305 Queen Anne Ave N, Seattle, WA 98109
Macrina Bakery & Café
615 W McGraw St, Seattle, WA 98119

24. RAINIER BEACH

The neighborhood of Rainier Beach is located in the southeastern part of Seattle. The population is approximately 15,000 residents, 4.2 square miles and the zip code is 98118 and 98178.

ATTRACTIONS
Kubota Garden
9817 55th Ave S, Seattle, WA 98118
Pitchard Island Beach
8400 55th Ave S, Seattle, WA 98118
Rainier Beach Community Center and Pool
8825 Rainier Ave S, Seattle, WA 98118
Henderson Street Park
8802 Seward Park Ave S, Seattle, WA 98118

Beer Sheva Park
8650 55th Ave S, Seattle, WA 98118
Rainier Beach Urban Farm and Wetlands
5813 S Cloverdale St, Seattle, WA 98118.

PUBLIC TRANSIT

Bus Route: The King County Metro Bus provides route 7, route 9, route 106 and route 107

Light Rail: The Sound Transit connects Rainier Beach to other parts of the city within the greater Seattle area. The Link Light Rail also connects rainier Beach Station to downtown Seattle and Sea-Tac Airport.

Bikeshare: There is a bikeshare program like Lime, Spin, JUMP (by Uber) which are all accessible through their mobile application service.

FOOD CUISINE

Redwing Café
9272 57th Ave S, Seattle, WA 98118
King Donut
9232 Rainier Ave S, Seattle, WA 98118
Bamboo Garden
9140 Rainier Ave S, Seattle, WA 98118
Nate's Wings and Waffles
9261 57th Ave S, Seattle, WA 98118
Emerald City Fish & Chips
3756 Rainier Ave S, Seattle, WA 98118
Taqueria El Sabor de Mexico

4019 Rainier Ave S, Seattle, WA 98118
The Green Plate
9232 Rainier Ave S, Seattle, WA 98118

25. RAVENNA/ BRYANT

The neighborhood of Ravenna is located in the northeastern region of Seattle. It is bordered by Roosevelt to the west, Wedgewood to the north, Bryant to the east and University district to the south. The population is about 12,000 residents, the land area is 1.2 square miles and the zip code is 98105.

Bryant is a neighborhood located in northeast region of Seattle known for its quiet streets and family-friendly atmosphere. The population of Bryant is approximately 6,000 residents, the land area is 0.9 square miles and the zip code is 98115.

ATTRACTIONS
Ravenna Park
5520 Ravenna Ave NE, Seattle, WA 98105
Cowen Park
5849 15th Ave NE, Seattle, WA 98105
University Village
2623 NE University Village St, Seattle, WA 98105
Third Place Books
6504 20th Ave NE, Seattle, WA 98115, Seattle, WA 98105
Seattle Public Library-Northeast Branch
6801 35th Ave NE, Seattle, WA 98115
Ravenna Eckstein Community Center
6535 Ravenna Ave NE, Seattle, WA 98115

Bryant Park
4103 NE 65th St, Seattle, WA 98115
View Ridge Playfield
4408 NE 70th St, Seattle, WA 98115

PUBLIC TRANSIT

Bus Route: In Ravenna the King Metro County Bus service routes 45, route 62, route 71. While in Bryant the King Metro Bus service routes 62, route 71 and route 75.

Light Rail: The University of Washington Station is located south of Ravenna 3720 Montlake Blvd NE, Seattle, WA 98195 with service to Northgate and Angle Lake passing through downtown Seattle.

Trail: The Burke-Gilman is a 27-mile multi-purpose trail located near Ravenna providing a picturesque view and safe route for cyclists and pedestrians.

Bikeshare: There is a bikeshare program like Lime and JUMP (by Uber) which are both accessible through their mobile application service.

FOOD CUISINE

Ravenna Brewing Company
5408 26th Ave NE, Seattle, WA 98105
Varlamos Pizzeria
3617 NE 45th St, Seattle, WA 98105
Pair
5501 30th Ave NE, Seattle, WA 98105
Sushi Katsu
4623 25th Ave NE, Seattle WA 98105

Café Campagne
1600 Post Alley, Seattle, WA 98101
Sunflower Café
5306 25th Ave NE, Seattle, WA 98105
Bryant Corner Café
3118 NE 65th St, Seattle, WA 98115
Metropolitan Market
5250 40th Ave NE, Seattle, WA 98105
Sand Point Grill
5520 35th Ave NE, Seattle, WA 98105
Tavern Law
1406 12th Ave, Seattle, WA 98122
Pizzalicious
5034 25th Ave NE, Seattle, WA 98105

26. ROXHILL/ WESTWOOD

The Roxhill neighborhood located in western Seattle with a suburban feel and family-friendly atmosphere. The population is about 7,000 residents, the land area is 1,3 square miles and the zip code is 98126.

Westwood neighborhood is located in western Seattle and is primarily residential with a community-oriented atmosphere. The population of Westwood is approximately 7,000 residents, the land area is 1,4 square miles and the zip code is 98126.

ATTRACTIONS
Roxhill Park
9650 29th Ave SW, Seattle, WA 98126
Westwood Village

2600 SW Barton St, Seattle, WA 98126
Camp Long
6200 35th Ave SW, Seattle, WA 98126
High Point Park
6400 Sylvan Way SW, Seattle, WA 98126
Westwood Park
2600 SW Barton St, Seattle, WA 98126
Burien Town Square Park
400 SW 152nd St, Burien, WA 98166

PUBLIC TRANSIT

Bus Route: The King County Metro bus route provides route 21, route 22, route 128. The bus route in Westwood have route 21, route 22 and route 120.

Bikeshare: There is a bikeshare program such as Lime and JUMP (by Uber) which can be accessed to their mobile application service.

FOOD CUISINE

Huarachitos Cocina Mexicana
9644 16th Ave SW, Seattle, WA 98106 **Buddha Ruksa**
3520 SW Genesee St, Seattle, WA 98126 **Harry's Chicken Joint**
6032 California Ave SW, Seattle, WA 98136
The Westy Sports & Spirits 7908 35th Ave SW, Seattle, WA 98126.

27. SEWARD PARK

The Seward Park neighborhood located in southeastern region of Seattle. It is popular for its greenery, recreational opportunities and community-oriented atmosphere. The population is approximately 8,000 residents, the land area is 1.5 square miles and the zip code is 98118.

ATTRACTIONS
Seward Park
5900 Lake Washington Blvd S, Seattle, WA 98118
Seward Park Community Center
5900 Lake Washington Blvd S, Seattle, WA 98118
Seward Park Audubon center
5902 Lake Washington Blvd S, Seattle, WA 98118

PUBLIC TRANSIT
Bus Route: The King County Metro Bus has services to route 7, route 8, route 9, route 50.

Bikeshare: There is a bikeshare program like Lime and JUMP (by Uber) which are accessible through their mobile application service.

28. SOUTHLAKE UNION/ DENNY TRIANGLE

The neighborhood of South Lake Union is located in northwest region of Seattle. It is known for its rapid growth, innovative tech scene and waterfront scenery. The population is approximately 12,000 residents, the land area is 1.5 square miles and the zip code is 98109.

WANDERING SEATTLE: A CULTURE ODYSSEY

Denny Triangle is a neighborhood in located in the Northwest Seattle, specifically in the Central area of the city often known as the "heartbeat" of the city. The population of Denny Triangle is approximately 9,000 residents, the land area is 0.5 square miles and the zip code is 98109.

ATTRACTIONS

Lake Union Park
860 Terry Ave N, Seattle, WA 98109
Museum of History & Industry (MOHAI)
860 Terry Ave N, Seattle, WA 98109
South Lake Union Discovery Center
800 Fairview Ave N, Seattle, WA 98109
The Center for Wooden Boats
1010 Valley St, Seattle, WA 98109
Gas Works Parks
2101 N Northlake Way, Seattle WA 98103
Amazon Spheres
2117 7th Ave, Seattle, WA 98109
Seattle Center
400 Broad St, Seattle, WA 98109
Fremont Bridge
N 34th St, Seattle, WA 98103
Denny Park
100 Dexter Ave N, Seattle, WA 98109
Westlake Center
400 Pine St, Seattle, WA 98101
Seattle Art Museum (SAM)
1300 1st Ave, Seattle, WA 98101
The Crocodile
2200 2nd Ave, Seattle, WA 98121
Pike Place Market
85 Pike St, Seattle, WA 98101

PUBLIC TRANSIT

Bus Route: The King County Metro bus has service in South Lake Union has route 8, route 12, route 40, route 43 and route 70. While the Denny Triangle has route 8, route 40, route 70, route 43 and route 10.

Light Rail: The Westlake Station offers services from University of Washington to Angle Lake with stops in downtown Seattle.

Bikeshare: There is a bikeshare program like Lime and Spin which are both accessible through their mobile application service.

FOOD CUISINE
Nijo Sushi
500 1st Ave N, Seattle, WA 98109,
Serious Pie
316 Virginia St, Seattle, WA 98101,
The Pink Door
1919 Post Alley, Seattle, WA 98101,
Café Campagne
1600 Post Alley, Seattle, WA 98101
Mediterranean Market
1503 1st Ave, Seattle, WA 98101
Sweetgreen
404 Pine St, Seattle, WA 98101
The 5-Point Café
415 Cedar St, Seattle, WA 98101
Molly Moon's Homemade Ice Cream
1000 East Pike St, Seattle, WA 98122
Tom Douglas Brave Horse Tavern

JORDAN BREED

310 Terry Ave N, Seattle, WA 98109
Mamma Melina Ristorante
1040 2nd Ave, Seattle, WA 98101
Nong's Khao Man Gai
2200 6th Ave, Seattle, WA 98121
Sushi Katsu 2332 6th Ave, Seattle, WA 98121

29. SOUTH PARK

The neighborhood of South Park is located on the southern region of Seattle approximately 6 miles south of downtown Seattle. It has a rich cultural diversity with many Hispanic and immigrant communities. The population is about 4,000 residents, the land area is 1.5 square miles and the zip code is 98126.

ATTRACTIONS

South Park Community Center
8319 8th Ave S, Seattle, WA 98108
Duwamish River Park
7900 10th Ave S, Seattle, WA 98108
South Park Marina
8600 7th Ave S, Seattle, WA 98108
The South Park Bridge
14th Ave S, Seattle, WA 98108
The Park at South Park
1300 S Cloverdale St, Seattle, WA 98168
Duwamish Longhouse and Cultural Center
4705 W Marginal Way S, Seattle, WA 98106
South Park Market
2920 S 3rd St, Seattle, WA 98134

PUBLIC TRANSIT

Bus Route: The King County Metro Bus has routes 42, route 60 and route 128.

Bikeshare: There is a bikeshare program like Lime and JUMP (by Uber) which are accessible through their mobile application service.

FOOD CUISINE

La Huerta
8500 14th Ave S, Seattle, WA 98108
Pupuseria y Restaurant El Salvador
12820 1st Ave S, Seattle, WA 98168
South Park Bar & Grill
2940 S 4th Ave, Seattle, WA 98134
Noodle Boat
1120 S 2nd St, Seattle, WA 98134
Bite of Seattle
1120 S 2nd St, Seattle, WA 98134
South Park Café
1300 S Cloverdale St, Seattle, WA 98168

30. UNIVERSITY DISTRICT

The popular U district neighborhood is located North of downtown Seattle. It home to University of Washington, one of the largest Universities in the United States. The population in U district is approximately 24,000 residents, the land area is 1.2 square miles and the zip code is 98105.

ATTRACTIONS

University of Washington
4000 University Way NE, Seattle, WA 98195,
Burke Museum of Natural History and Culture
4303 Memorial Way NE, Seattle, WA 98195
Husky Stadium
3800 Montlake Blvd NE, Seattle, WA 98195
University Village
2613 NE 46th St, Seattle, WA 98105
The Ave (University Way NE) University Way NE, Seattle, WA 98105
The Henry Art Gallery 4100 15th Ave NE, Seattle, WA 98195

PUBLIC TRANSIT

Bus Route: The King County Metro Bus has service route 25, route 43, route 66 and route 70.

Light Rail: The nearby station at University of Washington serves the University District with service to downtown Seattle, the SeaTac and other neighborhoods.

Bikeshare: There is a bikeshare program like Lime, JUMP (by Uber) and is accessible through their mobile application service.

FOOD CUISINE
Thai Tom
4543 University Way NE, Seattle, WA 98105
Pasta & Co.
4544 University Way NE, Seattle WA 98105
Los Agaves
4535 University Way NE, Seattle, WA 98105
Veggie Grill
5220 University Way NE, Seattle, WA 98105
The Cafe at the Henry Art Gallery
4100 15th Ave NE, Seattle, WA 98195

31. WALLINGFORD

The neighborhood of Wallingford is located North of downtown Seattle. It is popular for its residential charm, local shops and strong community network and is bordered by Green Lake to the North and University district to the South. The population is about 17,000 residents, the land area is approximately 2.2 square miles and the zip code is 98103.

ATTRACTIONS
Gas Works Park
2102 N Northlake Way, Seattle WA 98103
Wallingford Center
1815 N 45th St, Seattle, WA 98103
Meridian Park
500 Meridian Ave N, Seattle, WA 98103
Woodland Park Zoo
5500 Phinney Ave N, Seattle, WA 98103

PUBLIC TRANSIT
Bus Route: The King County Metro Bus service route 26, route 44, route 16 and route 40.

Bikeshare: There is a bikeshare program like Lime, JUMP (by Uber) and is accessible through their mobile application service.

FOOD CUISINE
Bacco Café
4918 25th Ave NE, Seattle, WA 98105
Burgermaster
1325 N 45th St, Seattle, WA 98103
Mamma Melina Ristorante

1702 N 45th St, Seattle, WA 98103
Morsel
1706 N 45th St, Seattle, WA 98103
Fremont Brewing Company
1050 N 34th St, Seattle, WA 98103

32. WEDGEWOOD/ VIEW RIDGE

The neighborhood of Wedgewood is located at Northeast Seattle. It is known for its tranquil environment, green spaces and community feel. The population is about 10,000 residents, the land area is 1.75 square miles and zip codes are 98115 and 98105.

View Ridge is a residential neighborhood in Northeast Seattle known for beautiful scenery and family-friendly atmosphere. The population is about 7,000 residents, the land area is 1.2 square miles and the zip code is 98105 and 98115.

ATTRACTIONS
Dahl Playfield
7700 25th Ave NE, Seattle, WA 98115
University Prep
8000 25th Ave NE, Seattle, WA 98115
Wedgwood Rock
Near 28th Ave NE and NE 72nd St, Seattle, WA 98115
Seattle Public Library-Northeast Branch
6801 35th Ave NE, Seattle, WA 98115
View Ridge Playfield
4408 NE 70th St, Seattle, WA 98115
Warren G. Magnuson Park
7400 Sand Point Way NE, Seattle, WA 98115

Sand Point Country Club
8333 55th Ave NE, Seattle, WA 98115
University Village
2623 NE University Village St, Seattle, WA 98105
Seattle's Children's Hospital
4800 Sand Point Way NE, Seattle, WA 98105

PUBLIC TRANSIT

Bus Route: The King County Metro Bus route for Wedgewood is route 62, route 71, route 372. While for View Ridge the bus route is route 62, route 75 and route 372.

Bikeshare: There is a bikeshare program like Lime and JUMP (by Uber) which are both accessible through their mobile application service.

FOOD CUISINE

Wedgwood Broiler
8230 35th Ave NE, Seattle, WA 98115
Miyabi Sushi
7201 35th Ave NE, Seattle, WA 98115
Caffe Vita
5021 25th Ave NE, Seattle, WA 98105
La Fonda
9125 35th Ave NE, Seattle, WA 98115
The Olive Tree
6807 35th Ave NE, Seattle, WA 98115
Bakery Nouveau
1435 E 70th St, Seattle, WA 98115
Squirrel Chaser Bakery
1316 NE 50th St, Seattle, WA 98105
Pagliacci Pizza
7311 35th Ave NE, Seattle, WA 98115

Taqueria El Asadero
1001 NE 63rd St, Seattle, WA 98115
Kizuki Ramen & Izakaya
7501 35th Ave NE, Seattle, WA 98115

33. WEST SEATTLE JUNCTION/GENESEE HILL

The West Seattle Junction neighborhood is located primarily around the intersection of California Avenue SW and SW Alaska Street. It serves as a commercial hub with various shops, restaurants and community spaces.

Genesee Hill is a quiet residential area with a mix of beauty and community amenities and is located in the West of Seattle. The population is 6,000 residents, the land area is 0.7 square miles and the zip code is 98126.

ATTRACTIONS
Early Street Records & Café
4559 California Ave SW, Seattle, WA 98116
Morgan Junction Park
6413 California Ave, SW, Seattle, WA 98136
Alaska Junction Park
4750 California Ave SW, Seattle, WA 98116
Genesee Park
4320 S Genesee St, Seattle, WA 98166
Camp Long
5200 35th Ave SW, Seattle, WA 98126
West Seattle Golf Course
4470 35th Ave SW, Seattle, WA 98126

PUBLIC TRANSIT

Bus Route: The King County Metro Bus route in West Seattle Junction is served by route 21, route 22, route 50, route 56.

While Genesee Hill there is route 21, route 22 and route 50.

Bikeshare: There is a bikeshare program like Lime and JUMP (by Uber) which are both accessible by mobile application service.

FOOD CUISINE

Easy Street Records & Café
4559 California Ave SW, Seattle, WA 98116
Jolly Roger Taproom
5510 California Ave SW, Seattle, WA 98136
Mamma Melina Ristorante
4759 California Ave SW, Seattle, WA 98116
The Seattle Fish Guys
4741 California Ave SW, Seattle, WA 98116
Starbucks
4721 California Ave SW, Seattle, WA 98116
The West Seattle Golf Course Café
4470 35th Ave SW, Seattle 98126.

REFERENCES
Seattle Department of Neighborhoods/Snapshots
Wikipedia/Neighborhoods in Seattle

WANDERING SEATTLE: A CULTURE ODYSSEY

Seattle City Council Districts

ABOUT THE AUTHOR JORDAN BREED

Jordan is a passionate traveler deeply connected to the city's rich history and diverse neighborhoods. He views each journey as a learning experience, seeking to understand the world through the lens of culture, architecture, and local lifestyles. His writing reflects a blend of practical insights and a deep appreciation for the city's unique offerings, aiming to provide readers with a comprehensive introduction to Seattle's neighborhoods.

Milton Keynes UK
Ingram Content Group UK Ltd.
UKHW040836021124
450589UK00001B/53